# When People Die

## Pete Sanders and Steve Myers

Aladdin / Watts
London • Sydney

© Aladdin Books Ltd 2004

Designed and produced by
Aladdin Books Ltd
28 Percy Street
London W1T 2BZ

New edition
first published in
Great Britain in 2004 by
Franklin Watts
96 Leonard Street
London EC2A 4XD

ISBN 0 7496 5495 3

Original edition published as
What Do You Know About –
Death and Dying

Editor
Katie Harker

Designer
Flick, Book Design & Graphics
Simon Morse

Illustrator
Mike Lacey

Picture Research
Brian Hunter Smart

# CONTENTS

## How to use this book

The books in this series deal with issues that may affect the lives of many young people.

● Each book can be read by a young person alone, or together with an adult.

● Issues raised in the storyline are further discussed in accompanying text.

● A list of practical ideas is given in the 'What can we do?' section at the end of the book.

● Organisations and helplines are listed for additional information and support.

# INTRODUCTION

" I couldn't believe that she was gone.
Every day I woke to a sinking feeling when
I remembered that she really wasn't
going to come back. "

**Death is a natural part of the cycle of life. However, many people find the subject of death very hard to talk about, because it means confronting issues and emotions that they find difficult to deal with.**

This book will help you to find out more about what dying means. It looks at some of the feelings and issues that might be raised and the kinds of reaction people may show at the death of someone they are close to. Each chapter introduces a different aspect of the subject, illustrated by a continuing storyline. The characters in the story are involved in situations which affect many people in their everyday lives. After each episode, we stop and consider the issues raised, and open out the discussion. By the end of the book, you will understand more about the the effects of losing a loved one and be able to make your own choices and decisions about how to deal with the subject of death in your own life.

It's not like that, Sarah. When Patch died, you were very young and we didn't explain it very well.

Death isn't like going to sleep, Darling. Sleep helps your body to rest, so that it can work properly. Everybody needs sleep.

# DEATH

" Granny lived life to the full and was very active
until her last days. She died peacefully in her sleep.
It was the way she would have wanted to go. "

**Death is something we will all have to face at some point. It is not something to be feared. When someone dies their body stops working. This usually means that their heart stops beating, their brain no longer functions and they stop breathing.**

There are many different reasons for this happening. Most of us, especially when we are young, expect to follow the natural process of life and live to an old age. For a great many people, death comes as a result of the natural effects of age on the body. However, death can be caused by other factors, and does not just happen to elderly people. Accidents, or even the deliberate actions of another person, can cause death. Some people have taken their own lives because of great unhappiness. Someone's state of health throughout life can affect their likelihood of developing a condition that might prove fatal. This is why doctors and other people stress the need to look after yourself at all stages of your life by eating a healthy, balanced diet and getting plenty of exercise. Medical advances mean that many diseases that at one time would have resulted in a person's death can now be cured. However, certain illnesses remain incurable. These are sometimes called 'terminal illnesses'.

Today, better social conditions and a greater awareness of health issues mean that we tend to live to an older age.

## One day....

... Jenny Wright and her brother, David, met up with some friends after school to play.

Reluctantly, James joined them. Soon, they were all pretending to have a battle.

What's wrong, James? Aren't you coming in?

I don't feel like playing in there. It's creepy.

It's perfect for playing Space Wars. Come on, don't be a coward.

Missed me!

No I didn't, Rav. I shot you. You're dead.

A short while later, James realised he couldn't see his friends anymore. They were all hiding from him.

Wwhhhhhoooo!

Come on, you guys. This isn't funny.

Rachel suddenly leapt out from behind one of the gravestones, making James jump.

You idiot! You scared me. Anyhow, we shouldn't be playing in here. It isn't right.

We're not doing any harm.

Matt's right. Come on, let's play.

David ran off, chased by Jenny and Ravinder.

I got you, David!

Aaaarrrgh!

What do you think you are doing? This isn't a playground. You, get up. That's my son's grave. Don't you have any respect?

They all apologised and began to walk away. David felt really bad about what had happened.

5

He told the others to wait, and turned back to the woman.

That's ok. My Daniel was just the same. He would have been about your age now.

The woman told David her name was Mrs Salako. Her son had been killed in a car crash a year earlier.

I didn't mean to upset you. I wasn't thinking. Mum's always telling me about that. I'm really sorry.

My grandpa is buried over there. I don't understand why people have to die. It seems so unfair.

I know. The hospital did everything they could for Daniel, but in the end they couldn't save him.

David told Mrs Salako that his grandmother was very ill now.

She's lived with us since Grandpa died, but she's been in the hospital some of the time. I don't really know what's wrong with her, but I think it's worse than Mum and Dad are saying.

David, are you coming? We should be getting back.

David said goodbye to Mrs Salako and left with Jenny.

You shouldn't have been talking about Grandma like that. You didn't know that woman. You know that Mum and Dad have told us not to talk to strangers.

I know, but you and the others were there. I wanted to apologise.

Don't be so morbid. I'm sure Mum and Dad would have told us if there was anything seriously wrong.

I'm not so sure. They've been really secretive lately.

Mrs Salako seemed nice. She was telling me about her son dying. It made me think about Grandma. Maybe she's dying. I think she's really ill.

As they made their way home, Jenny began to wonder if David might be right.

No I didn't, Rav.
I shot you. You're dead.

**Like David and his friends, lots of young people enjoy playing games.** Often these are based on events from TV shows or films, and involve pretend violence where characters use imaginary weapons to 'kill' each other. Some adults worry about the effect these games can have on those who play them. They believe that they encourage young people to see violence as acceptable.

## The friends did not intend to upset Mrs Salako.

However, Mrs Salako thought that it was insensitive of them to play such a game in a cemetery, and that it showed a lack of respect for her dead son and the others buried there. When people die, they are no longer a part of the physical world around us. However, the memory of the dead person can be very important to friends and family. It can be distressing if others do not seem to respect it.

It is important to separate the fiction of the game from the facts of real life. Because we see so much 'pretend' death on TV, it can be tempting to think of death as something very remote. In films, characters often survive incidents that nobody could survive in reality. Some young people have been seriously injured trying to copy the kind of actions they have seen their favourite actors doing.

I'm sure Mum and Dad would have told us if there was anything seriously wrong.

**Jenny is starting to worry that her mum and dad may not be telling her the truth about Grandma.**
Adults often find it diffucult to talk about death, particularly to children. They may believe they are sparing young people unnecessary worry and pain. But not talking about a situation might cause much anxiety and may make it more difficult to deal with.

# DYING

" When I found out that Dad was dying I couldn't come to terms with it. He didn't look like he was ill. I thought the doctors must have made a mistake. "

**Death is the moment at which life ends. It can also mean the event or process that results in a person's death. This might happen very quickly or it may take a long time.**

People will sometimes say that they are not frightened of death itself, but that they are afraid of dying. They may see some ways of dying as 'worse' than others, perhaps because they involve some suffering for the dying person. The way in which a person dies might affect the reaction of other people to his or her death. Some people are told that they are going to die – perhaps because they have an illness that cannot be cured. When this happens, the effect on them and those close to them can be devastating. Everyone will react differently. Certain emotions, however, are common to many people. At first, there may be disbelief at the news, as people try to deny the truth of what they have been told. They may become angry, asking why this should happen to them or to someone they love. Most will experience periods of great sadness. It is not unusual to experience these emotions.

If someone knows that they are dying it does not necessarily prevent them from enjoying life.

## Two days later...

... Jenny and David's younger sister, Sarah, was helping Mrs Wright to prepare a meal.

Mrs Wright was surprised. She sat down at the table.

What's the matter with you two? You look very serious.

We want to ask you something.

We want to know what's really wrong with Grandma. She's much worse than she used to be.

Is she going to die?

Sarah, why don't you go and put your new video on, Darling? I want to speak to David and Jenny for a moment.

Sarah happily ran into the other room. Mrs Wright said she would speak to her later. David could tell she was close to tears.

David and Jenny were both very upset.

You know everyone has to die at some time. Your grandma has a serious illness. The doctors say they can't do any more for her. She's dying.

How long will she live?

Nobody knows, Darling. But she's going to need a lot of care and attention.

We'll look after her.

It's not as easy as that, I'm afraid. Your grandma will need more specialised care than we can give her at home. Your dad and I have been talking about trying to find her a place in a hospice.

They'll have the facilities to care really well for your grandma. You'll still be able to visit her whenever you want.

David and Jenny both asked what a hospice was. Mrs Wright explained.

## Later on....

... Sarah asked her parents what it meant to die. She had overheard David and Jenny talking.

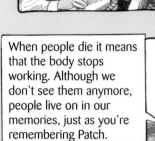

When my dog, Patch, got sick you told me he was going to sleep for a long time and I wouldn't be able to see him anymore. Is that what's going to happen to Grandma? What if I go to sleep and never wake up? What if I die, too?

It's not like that, Sarah. When Patch died, you were very young and we didn't explain it very well.

Death isn't like going to sleep, Darling. Sleep helps your body to rest so that it can work properly. Everybody needs sleep.

When people die it means that the body stops working. Although we don't see them anymore, people live on in our memories, just as you're remembering Patch.

Sarah asked a few more questions. Her mum and dad tried to answer them as honestly as possible.

Do you want to take Grandma's tray into her? She says she hasn't seen you lately.

I don't think I can go into her room. I don't want to see her. It makes me feel really uncomfortable.

## The next morning...

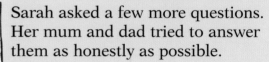

... David was preparing breakfast for Grandma.

I've brought you your breakfast, Grandma.

That's kind of you, Dear. Jenny, it's lovely to see you. Why don't you come in and sit on the bed and talk to me for a while?

I felt a bit like that at first. After we found out, it was odd – I didn't know whether to talk about it. But when I saw her I realised that she's still Grandma. You'll feel worse if you don't see her.

Eventually, Jenny did spend some time with Grandma. She was pleased she had overcome her worries.

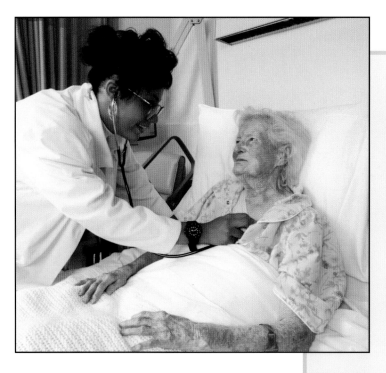

Your grandma will need more specialised care than we can give her at home.

**Many elderly people need special care to keep them well.**
Some people can be cared for at home. Others may need hospital treatment. People who are dying may be able to stay in a hospice for a short while before going back home, or until their death. Whatever the situation, someone who is dying deserves to be treated with dignity.

I don't think I can go into her room. I don't want to see her.

**Jenny is unsure how to treat Grandma.**
Some people's own fears about death can influence their behaviour. They might be afraid of upsetting the person and believe that they shouldn't cry or show any emotion. But someone who is dying will usually want you to treat them in just the same way as you always have done.

**Finding the right words to describe death can be difficult.**
It is very hard for some adults who are unsure how to discuss the issues with young people. Like Sarah, many younger children might easily misunderstand messages like 'he's gone to sleep' or 'she's gone away for a very long time'. This can be very confusing and frightening. Clear discussion of the subject can help to avoid any unnecessary fears and worries.

# HOW DO PEOPLE FEEL ABOUT DEATH?

> " I'm not frightened of death – I know that it comes to us all. But I do wonder what happens to us when we die. "

**People's attitudes towards death can vary a great deal. Because life is very precious to most of us, our feelings about death are sometimes surrounded by uncertainty and fear.**

Many people are reluctant to talk about the subject. They may fear that doing so somehow brings death nearer. Some see death as affecting only elderly people, so they think that it need not concern them. But facing up to the subject can help us to cope with our feelings and those of others around us, when we become directly affected by the death of someone close. Talking about death means confronting particular concerns, such as anxiety about what happens after death, worry about what will happen to those you love and a fear of being separated from them. People might also be afraid that dying involves physical pain, or that they will need someone else to look after them if they are very ill. However, many people are able to accept that dying is a natural part of life and not something to be afraid of. But this does not always mean that if someone close to them dies, their feelings will be any less strong or easier to deal with.

Some people enjoy the risks and excitement of taking part in 'death-defying' sports or pursuits.

## A few weeks later...

... in the playground, David and his friends were talking about a new boy who had arrived at school.

In another part of the playground, Rachel and Jenny were talking about Jenny's grandma.

That's Stefan. He's a refugee. He's just started in my class. I heard that both his parents had been killed. He's living with foster parents in this country now.

It must be awful. I've seen photographs of the fighting on the news, but it all seems so far away.

The people at the hospice are good, but I can't stand to see Grandma in so much pain.

I can't think how I'd feel if that happened to my family.

I don't think I could go through with it. I'd rather die quickly than suffer – I'd even ask the doctors to give me something to do it.

That's a terrible thing to say. Life's always got to be better than death, whatever the circumstances. What if the doctors were able to find a cure tomorrow?

The boys were passing and overheard Jenny and Rachel talking.

I read that in some countries it's legal for doctors to help people die, if there's no hope of them getting better and the person wants it to happen.

It depends on your religion, too. I don't think anyone has the right to take a life.

Everybody began to talk about how they felt.

Do you have to talk about death so much? I don't like it. It's tempting fate, or something.

Don't be silly! You're just superstitious.

Come on. Let's go over and see if Stefan wants to play with us.

The group went over to Stefan.

When he arrived home that evening, David found his mum going through some papers.

What are you doing, Mum? Are those Grandma's?

Yes. Your grandma asked me to go over everything to make sure it's all in order. She made a will, but it's been a while since she looked at it. Some things might need to be updated.

She made a will, but it's been a while since she looked at it. Some things might need to be updated.

**Mrs Wright is making certain that her mother's will is in order.**
A will is a legal document that gives instructions in the event of your death – for example, details of who you want your money or property to go to. Making a will enables other people to respect your wishes and can help to avoid misunderstandings. A will can also help to ensure that your loved ones will be supported financially when you die. Many people carry donor cards so that in the event of their death, doctors can use their organs to help patients who need a transplant.

## Stefan's parents have been killed in a war.

The death of a parent or guardian can be bewildering for young people because it may mean practical changes in who looks after them. At an early age, Stefan has had to come to terms with the death of his family. This has not been caused by illness or old age, but by war. It can be especially difficult to understand and accept the death of someone close when it has been caused by the action of another person, either deliberately or accidently.

I'd rather die quickly than suffer – I'd even ask the doctors to give me something to do it.

**Rachel thinks that she would prefer to be helped to die rather than to live in pain.**
Causing the death of someone, with his or her consent, to avoid further suffering, is called euthanasia. Euthanasia is illegal in most countries, although in some it is legal under very special circumstances. There is much debate about the morality of euthanasia. Many people believe that, no matter what, nobody has the right to end a life or take any action that would lead to another person's death. Others believe that each person should have the right to choose, depending on his or her own situation.

# WHAT HAPPENS AFTER YOU DIE?

> It can be comforting to think that you go somewhere else when you die. My belief in an afterlife has helped me to come to terms with the death of my mother.

**There are many different ideas about what happens to us after we die, but there is no right or wrong answer. Some people have very strong views that are often based on their religion or culture.**

According to some people, we are all made up of two parts – the physical body and an invisible element, sometimes called the spirit or soul. It is this that they think is the most important part of our being, which makes us what we are and which gives us our personality. They believe that, although the body decays after death, the soul or immortal spirit of the person is 'released' and continues to exist in some way. Many people talk about heaven

and hell – places to which the soul is sent, depending on whether a person was 'good' or 'bad' while alive. Some people and religions talk about reincarnation, believing that the soul is reborn as another person or creature. Others do not think anything happens to us when we die – that it is simply the end. You may have your own opinions about the subject. Many people feel very strongly about their beliefs. It is important to remember that everyone is entitled to his or her own view.

Many religious followers, like members of the Russian Orthodox Church (right), believe very strongly in an 'afterlife' – that the soul continues to exist although the body is no longer part of the physical world.

15

## A few weeks later...

... Jenny and David were visiting Grandma in the hospice. They began to talk about Grandpa.

I can remember when we used to stay with you. Grandpa used to tell these fantastic stories.

Yeah. They were supposed to be bedtime stories, but they were so good, we wouldn't go to sleep!

Grandpa could always tell a good story.

## That weekend...

... Jenny and David decided to visit their grandpa's grave.

It's horrible to think Grandma's going to be buried here soon.

I'm going to miss her so much. What do you think happens to you when you die? Do you think Grandma and Grandpa will be together again somewhere?

I'd like to think so. Nobody really knows what happens to you, do they? Do you think we have a soul that leaves our body when we die?

So did I. I thought he was watching out for me. It felt good, but also a bit odd, as if he'd know if I ever did anything wrong.

I don't know but I don't think death can just be the end of everything. I used to think Grandpa was somewhere watching me.

The boy said he was Daniel's brother, Chris. They all started chatting.

David had noticed a boy standing by Daniel's grave. He went over to him.

I come here every week, and talk to Daniel. I don't like to stay too late, though. I wouldn't want to be here when it's dark, in case there are any ghosts.

I was only trying to scare you. It was a silly thing to do.

We are going to get a burger. Do you want to come with us?

Don't be silly. There are no such things as ghosts. That's just in stories.

Some people believe in them, though. There are all kinds of ideas about what happens when you die.

Chris accepted. They all left to go into town.

16

I can remember when we used to stay with you. Grandpa used to tell these fantastic stories.

**David and Jenny have enjoyed talking about Grandpa with Grandma.**

Remembering someone who has died is very important to most people. It may be a memory of a special time spent together, a favourite photograph, a particular place, or even a smell, which calls to mind something about the person. Some people, however, find it difficult to be around things that remind them of a person who has died. Memories can make you feel both happy and sad. Sometimes people tend to concentrate only on the happy ones. But there is nothing wrong with remembering sad times or things you did not like about the person. Nor is there anything wrong in enjoying your own life – you do not need to feel guilty about this.

I used to think Grandpa was somewhere watching me.

**Like David and Jenny, many people feel that someone who has died still cares for and protects them.**

It can be comforting to think that a person who has died is still part of your life. At times we might think that they can see everything that we are doing. This can be reassuring. But sometimes adults will tell young people this is in order to try to control their behaviour. This is not a good idea and can be very frightening, especially for younger children.

**Chris has tried to frighten the others by talking about ghosts.**

You have probably read stories or watched films about places that are supposed to be haunted by the spirits of dead people. Some people believe in ghosts; others do not. Unusual events are sometimes said to be caused by spirits. It may be that the strength of our imagination is responsible for some unexplained events. Nothing has been proved either way. Whatever the case, it is not something to be frightened of.

# REACTIONS TO LOSS

> " *When I heard the news I felt like my world had fallen apart. At first I couldn't cry. I couldn't eat or sleep and I didn't feel like seeing anybody for a few days.* "

**Losing somebody close, through death, is called 'bereavement'. People can have very different reactions to the loss of a loved one.**

It may depend on the individual and the relationship with the person who has died. The way that someone has died can also affect the way we react to the news, as can the age of both the deceased and the person being told about his or her death. Other factors may be the role of the dead person in people's lives, and what his or her death will mean in practical terms – if it means having to move, for example. Often the initial response is a feeling of shock. This may be more extreme if a death is sudden. But it can still be the case when a person has been ill for a long time and death had been expected at some point. Shock and numbness will usually then give way to grief. Our feelings often take us by surprise. Some people might appear to show no immediate reaction but this does not necessarily mean that they do not care or feel deeply. Every person has an individual response to sad news.

The loss of someone close can cause many different and confusing emotions. Some of these may be influenced by the type and strength of the relationship you shared.

18

## A month later...

... Jenny and David came down to breakfast to find their mum crying.

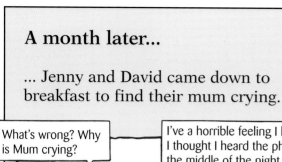

What's wrong? Why is Mum crying?

I've a horrible feeling I know. I thought I heard the phone ring in the middle of the night. It's Grandma, isn't it?

I'm afraid so.

She took a turn for the worse last night. We asked Mrs Baker from next door to stay with you while we went to the hospice. She died an hour after we arrived.

No! Grandma can't be dead.

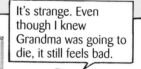

David began to to cry. Mr Wright sat them down and explained what had happened.

You should have woken us up. We could have gone with you.

I never said goodbye or told her how much I loved her. I should have gone to visit her more. Now I'll never see her again.

I'm sorry, Darling. We did what we thought was best. She died very peacefully.

It's strange. Even though I knew Grandma was going to die, it still feels bad.

I know your grandpa died suddenly, and that was an awful shock. This is different. But I think getting over it is going to be just as difficult. I can't believe she's gone.

I feel so sad, but I can't cry.

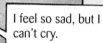

Jenny and David realised how their mum must be feeling. After a while, everyone was able to talk more calmly.

Sarah had been standing just outside the door. She suddenly burst into tears and ran upstairs.

Mr Wright told Jenny that not everybody cries when they are sad. He said it can take time for feelings to sink in.

The next day at school, Rachel told Jenny she was sorry to hear of her grandma's death.

Sarah, darling. It's ok.

I'll go. I didn't realise she was listening. She shouldn't have heard about it like that.

It sounds awful, but when my grandma died, I didn't really feel sad. She lived miles away, and I never saw much of her.

It's different for me. Grandma lived with us for a long time. We were very close.

> I never said goodbye or told her how much I loved her.

**Jenny is upset because she feels that she didn't have the chance to say goodbye.**
This can be hard to deal with whether death is sudden or expected. You may be left feeling guilty and sad because of things you did, or did not, say or do before someone's death. It is important to remember that you are not in any way to blame for the person's death.

## Many people cry when someone they were close to has died.

But not everyone cries, and this does not mean that their feelings for the person are any less strong. Some will cry more than others, and at different times. Crying is sometimes wrongly thought of as a sign of weakness. You may have heard it said that boys and men should not cry. This is not true. It's okay to cry and it's okay not to cry. People express their feelings in very different ways.

> Your grandpa died suddenly, and that was an awful shock. This is different but I think getting over it is going to be just as difficult.

**The way in which people react to the news of a death can vary according to the situation.**
When death is unexpected, the shock might be overwhelming at first. When someone has been ill for a long time, those close to him or her may have had time to adjust and prepare themselves for the news. Sometimes people can feel a sense of relief, especially if the person was suffering or in a great deal of pain. This can be a difficult emotion to accept. There is no right or wrong way to react. However you react to the news, it does not mean that your grief is any less real or sincere than someone else's.

# FUNERALS AND RITUALS

Focusing on arrangements for the funeral really helped us to get through the first few days. We put all our energy into organising a good send-off and worked together in our grief.

**It is important for many people to pay their last respects and to say goodbye to the person who has died. A funeral is an official ceremony at which people can do this. It usually involves burial of the body or 'cremation', when the body is burned.**

In most countries, before a funeral is able to take place, a death certificate will be issued, stating the cause of death. This will have been determined by an official such as the person's doctor or an authorised medical examiner, who may sometimes need to do tests to find out the exact cause. The nature of a

funeral or ritual to mark the death of someone can depend on several factors, such as the person's country, culture or religion. It may involve a religious ceremony, or a person's friends talking about what they loved about him or her. Although a funeral is often a sad occasion, it can have a positive side. For many, it is a chance to honour and to say goodbye to someone they cared about. It is also a time when friends and family can offer each other support and understanding.

In some cultures, wearing black is considered a sign of respect for the dead person. In others, it is traditional for relatives to dress in white.

21

## The funeral was to take place a few days later.

At the service, the family cried a lot. Afterwards, Jenny tried to comfort her mum.

Sarah's too young to understand what's happening. It would be too upsetting for her. She's going to Mrs Baker's for the afternoon.

Are you both sure you want to go? I won't be upset if you decide you'd rather stay here.

No. We want to go.

Come on, Mum. Don't cry. I can't bear to see you so upset.

Mum'll be alright, Jenny. She needs to cry now. Don't worry.

It was like saying goodbye again, wasn't it?

That's part of what a funeral's all about. It gives people a chance to remember someone and think about them.

## The next day...

... At school, his friends asked David about the funeral.

I've never been to one. I don't think I ever want to go.

It wasn't so bad, although everyone cried a lot. Grandma was buried next to Grandpa.

I don't want to be buried when I die. I want to be cremated, like my uncle was.

He has a golden plaque in a place called a garden of remembrance. I think it would be nicer than being in the graveyard, with all those weird stones and things.

In my religion, everyone who dies is cremated. We don't bury people.

The ancient Egyptians used to be buried with all kinds of treasures. They thought they might need them in the next world. I like that idea.

What about reincarnation? Some people believe you come back as someone or something else after death. I don't think it's true, do you?

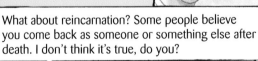

Who knows? Are you coming to play football? Are you coming to the park after school, David?

The friends began to talk about different beliefs.

David said no. He was meeting Chris Salako. The two of them had become good friends.

Sarah's too young to understand what's happening. It would be upsetting for her.

**Sarah's parents think it's best that she doesn't go to the funeral.**

Younger children may not always fully understand the significance of funerals. Some might be confused or even frightened by what happens. Although adults often believe they are protecting them by not allowing them to attend, some young people might be upset at being excluded. They may want the same chance as everyone else to say goodbye. Each situation needs to be judged individually.

Mum'll be alright, Jenny. She needs to cry now. Don't worry.

**Jenny hates to see her mum upset. But her dad realises that she needs to express her grief.**

A funeral is a time when most people will experience intense emotions. It is never easy to see those you love suffering, and your immediate reaction might be to want to help stop their pain. But this is not always possible. Funerals can bring out feelings that people have been bottling up because they are so difficult to face. Telling someone not to cry will not help them to deal with those feelings. A funeral is a time when most people will experience intense emotions.

**People symbolise death in different ways.**

This depends on religious and cultural beliefs, and such things as family traditions. Some cultures have annual celebrations or ceremonies at which the spirits of the dead are honoured with gifts. These may be very happy occasions. Many people commemorate the deceased with a plaque or headstone.

23

# GRIEF

" It was a very difficult time. On the outside, I seemed to be coping and everyone said how well I was doing. But on the inside I was grieving terribly. "

**Coming to terms with the fact that someone close to you has died can take a long time. Many people will experience grief after a bereavement. This is often a mixture of strong physical and emotional reactions. It may also be called 'mourning'.**

The responses can be similar to those of someone who has been told that he or she is dying. People may be unable to believe what has happened, or they may become depressed and angry. Others feel that their own life is no longer worth living. They might have difficulty sleeping or have headaches. Most people experience many different feelings at the same time. Someone may appear to be coping, then might suddenly break down in tears. They may cry a lot or show no interest in what is going on around them. It can seem as if there are no limits to how terrible you are feeling, or as though the grief will never end. It can help to talk about your feelings with others. Very young children might not be able to put their emotions into words; instead, they may act them out. It is very important for everybody to have the chance to grieve.

When some people are grieving, they may seem to lose their temper more quickly than usual. This is often because they are trying to cope with so many confusing emotions.

# One weekend...

... David and Jenny met Chris and his mum in town. Mrs Salako asked how they were both feeling.

We're ok. It's Mum I'm worried about. She's taken Grandma's death really badly.

It's been two months now since she died. I thought Mum would feel better by now.

But Daniel was very young and he died in an accident. Grandma was quite old, and we knew she was going to die.

It's not that simple, David. It can take a long time to get over a death. It's more than a year since Daniel died, and I still cry about him sometimes.

That doesn't necessarily make it easier when it happens. Losing a child is terrible, but anyone's death, no matter how old they are or how they died, can be difficult to cope with.

Mrs Salako said that it was not always possible to know how grief would affect people.

## The following weekend...

... Jenny and David invited some friends over. Chris arrived first.

Good to finally meet you, Chris.

What are you up to, Sarah? Are you knitting?

Those are Grandma's needles. She used to love to knit. I'll teach you to knit properly if you like, Sarah.

I don't want to talk about Grandma. I don't like Grandma. She didn't love me or she wouldn't have gone away.

David apologised to Chris and they all went out into the garden.

Sarah threw down the needles and ran out of the room.

Sorry about that.

That's ok. I know how Sarah's feeling. When Daniel died, I used to hate him for leaving me. Mum missed Daniel so much – for a while it was like I didn't exist.

It took Mum a long time to come to terms with his death. Things are better now, and we talked about it a lot. But I still get angry sometimes.

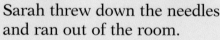

It's only natural. I still get upset about Grandma. Look, here are the others.

They went over to join their friends.

25

It's more than a year since Daniel died, and I still cry about him sometimes.

**As David knows, the death of a baby or child can be particularly difficult to come to terms with.**

The death of someone at a young age may seem unfair, because the person has been cheated of the chance to grow up. Parents and brothers and sisters may be devastated by the loss and find it difficult to accept. It can be very hard for the other children in the family if their parents are so distressed that they seem to be ignoring them. But the grief their parents are experiencing may temporarily seem to block out everything else. Parents may be feeling guilty about their child's death, believing that, as parents, they should have been capable of doing something to prevent it, even when there was nothing they could have done.

## Mrs Salako knows that there is no set time at which grief begins or ends.

How you cope with your grief will depend on your own personality, the circumstances of the death and the support you receive from others.

When Daniel died, I used to hate him for leaving me.

**Chris has said that he hated his brother after he died, because of the effect that his death had on his mum.**
Death forces changes in people's lives. It is normal for people to experience feelings of anger towards the dead person. They may blame him or her for leaving. It is not unusual for people who are very upset to say and do things that they may not really mean or might later regret.

# LEARNING TO COPE

> *It felt very strange to laugh again. It made me feel guilty. But then I realised that Dad wouldn't want me to be sad all the time – the daughter he knew wasn't miserable.*

**Given time, most people come to terms with even the most difficult of feelings. Going on with your own life does not mean that you have to forget about the person who has died, or that you are betraying him or her in any way.**

We cannot stop our own lives because of the death of someone else. Nor is it likely that the deceased would want us to. It can be useful to talk about how you feel, and perhaps to discuss the dead person with others who knew them. Some have found that keeping busy helps them to cope with their grief. There is nothing wrong with this, as long as they do not simply bottle up their emotions or try to avoid having to face them. As people's feelings of grief become easier to bear, they may sometimes feel guilty about lighter moments, making new friends or having a good time. But there is no reason why anyone should feel that it is wrong to enjoy life. Mourning does not have to consist of only unhappy moments, even though at first it can seem as though the sadness might never go away.

Feeling sad is a natural part of the grieving process. But it needn't stop you from living your life to the full. The person who has died would not want you to stop doing the things that you enjoy, like going out with your friends.

... Jenny found David in his room, writing a letter.

It's a letter to Grandma. It would have been her birthday tomorrow.

I know. Why write a letter, though? It's not as though she can actually read it.

That's not the point. I still wanted to tell her how I felt. Anyway, you still talk to her sometimes. I've heard you.

I suppose I do. It just helps to talk about things, the way we used to when she was alive. I try to imagine what Grandma would say.

David finished his letter. He went to show it to his mum.

It's lovely, Darling. What a nice thing to do.

I did it because I was afraid of forgetting about Grandma. Sometimes, when I'm having a good time, I feel guilty.

I was very upset at first. I don't know where I'd have been without you two and your dad. But feelings do change gradually. It's okay to feel happy. Your grandma wouldn't have wanted you to be sad all the time.

Mrs Wright said that neither of them should feel guilty about enjoying themselves. They'd never forget Grandma.

Mrs Wright suggested they arrange to go out for a day the following weekend.

David and Jenny invited Chris and Mrs Salako and some of their other friends along too. They all went to the park.

Your mum seems a lot happier now.

It was Grandma's birthday last week and that was a bit difficult, but otherwise things are much better now.

We all went to Grandma's grave and took some flowers. It was sad, but quite nice too.

I know. Special occasions are always hard. Come on, you guys. Help me get these boats in the water.

It was Grandma's birthday last week and that was a bit difficult.

**Special times, such as birthdays or holidays, may bring back the memory of a person who has died.** Sometimes this can bring the same kind of emotions you felt immediately after their death. This is natural and will become easier to handle with time. Most people are eventually able to separate the memory of the person from their grief. Remembering people is important and can give a lot of pleasure. But not thinking about someone all the time doesn't make that person or their memory any less important to you.

I don't know where I'd have been without you two and your dad.

**Mrs Wright knows that, through this difficult time, it is important to have the help and support of others.**
After a person has died, you may think you are not able to talk to the people you would normally turn to, because they are also grieving. You may think that mentioning the person's name will upset people. But as long as everyone is willing, sharing your grief with others who are feeling the same way can help you all. It can be comforting to talk about your loss, and although you may find that you cry, it can help to release your emotions.

**It is difficult when the person who has died is the one you really want to talk to about the way you are feeling.** Expressing emotions in practical ways, like David has done, by writing a letter or poem can help people to work through their grief or to say things they would have wanted the deceased to know. This can help especially if someone did not have the chance to say goodbye.

# WHAT CAN WE DO?

When Sam's brother died we didn't know what to say to him. We didn't want to upset him, and in a way we were grieving ourselves. When Sam raised the topic, I was only too pleased to help him.

**Having read this book, you will understand that death is a natural part of all our lives. You will know how important it is to express grief and to offer and receive the support needed.**

There may be times when you feel you do not know the right words to say. Just being there for people can help, or giving practical assistance, perhaps by cooking, shopping or looking after pets for people who are grieving. If you are experiencing feelings of grief yourself, you will know that these can be very difficult to handle, but that this should become easier with time. There is no need to feel that you cannot express your emotions. Talking to others about what you are going through can sometimes do the world of good.

**Talking honestly about death can help both children and adults to come to terms with losing a loved one.**

Finding the right words can be difficult, especially if you feel uncomfortable about discussing the issues, or are grieving yourself. Adults and children who have read this book together may find it helpful to share their thoughts and ideas about the issues raised. Many of the organisations listed below provide information, advice and support for both adults and children.

**The Befriending Network**
24-27 White Lion Street
London N1 9PD
Tel: 020 7689 2443
Fax: 020 7689 2421
Email:
info@befriending.net
Website:
www.befriending.net

**The Childhood Bereavement Trust**
Aston House
High Street
West Wycombe
High Wycombe
HP14 3AG
Tel: 01494 446 648
Helpline: 0845 357 1000
Email: enquiries@
childbereavement.org.uk
Website: www.
childbereavement.org.uk

**Childline**
45 Folgate Street
London
E1 6GL
Tel: 020 7650 3200
24-hour helpline:
0800 11 11
Textphone: 0800 400 222
Website:
www.childline.org.uk

**Cruse Bereavement Care**
Cruse House
126 Sheen Road
Richmond
Surrey TW9 1UR
Tel: 020 8939 9530
Helpline: 0870 167 1677
Email: helpline@
crusebereavementcare.org.uk
Website: www.
crusebereavementcare.org.uk

**The Rainbow Trust**
The Crypt
St Luke's Church
Sydney Street
London SW3 6NH
Tel: 020 7352 6522
Email: enquiries@
rainbowtrust.org.uk
Website:
www.rainbowtrust.org.uk

**The Samaritans**
The Upper Mill
Kingston Road
Ewell
Surrey KT17 2AF
Tel: 020 8394 8300
Helpline:
0845 7 90 90 90
Email:
admin@samaritans.org
Website:
www.samaritans.org.uk

**Winston's Wish**
The Clara Burgess Centre
Bayshill Road
Cheltenham
GL50 3AW
Tel: 01242 515157
Helpline:
0845 20 30 40 5
Email:
info@winstonswish.org.uk
Website:
www.winstonswish.org.uk

**Kids Help Line**
PO Box 376
Red Hill
Queensland 4059
Australia
Tel: +61 (0) 7 3369 1588
Fax: +61 (0) 7 3367 1266
Email:
admin@kidshelp.com.au
Website:
www.kidshelp.com.au

**Skylight**
PO Box 7309
Wellington South
New Zealand
Tel: +64 (04) 939 6759
Helpline: +64 0800 299 100
Email:
info@skylight-trust.org.nz
Website:
www.skylight.org.nz

# INDEX